LEAD

HOW TO LEAD

YOUR WAY

AT ANY LEVEL

UP

IRIS IRUMVA

Printed in the United Kingdom
St Helena's Road,
Southwark, London
SE16 2QY
www.thewisdomous.co
The Wisdomous Publishing
First Printing, 2023
ISBN: 978-1-7394792-0-6

To all the people out there who are hungry for growth, who are willing to bet on themselves no matter how many "No's" they get.

To anyone who has ever felt like their purpose is unclear or their potential is still up for grabs. This book is dedicated to you.

And to my parents, who raised me not to be mediocre but rather to be a person with grit and ambition. Thank you for being my rock and safety net in every step of my life's journey. I love you.

Table of Contents

Introduction

———

Spaghetti. When I was younger, I went by this moniker. I was given a label due to my petite stature and delicate look; at 16 years old, I weighed nearly 40 kilograms. Although I looked light on the outside, I was heavy on the inside, and I had a burning desire to do anything I set my mind to.

But life has a strange way of testing our beliefs and shattering the defenses we construct. My path to becoming a leader started with one of these unanticipated events.

During a course on leadership and management in my university class, a Kenyan professor, Njoroge, attempted to get our opinions on the subject. He asked us the often-debated question, "Do you think leaders are born[i] or made?"

I never considered myself a leader. The concept of leading and motivating people seemed far-fetched and unrealistic. I didn't see how someone like me, who didn't have the stereotypical traits of a leader, could make a difference.

Self-doubt had shattered my goals, and the weight of other people's opinions was crushing my small shoulders.

When Professor Njoroge asked his question, I froze and stayed quiet.

Everyone turned their heads to look at our two class leaders. I wondered if they were also born that way or had grown into it.

At that time, my classmates and I had little professional experience to confidently respond to what a leader was. We had a general, or rather vague, idea of leadership.

We knew what an academic leader looked like, and we instinctively looked toward him when Professor Njoroge asked his question. I'm talking about that "A" student who always seems to know as much as the professor.

They lead group studies and explain things more straightforwardly. And they are invited to every function because everyone wants to befriend them. I'm talking about that student you'd notice if they missed class and that student who was every professor's favorite person.

The other of our two class leaders was the popular leader. This student was never an "A" student. But they were the class's most opinionated and significant influencers for some reason. This was especially true when making critical decisions, voicing students' concerns, and organizing after-class events.

Professors didn't necessarily like this type of leader, but they all acknowledged the power of their influence.

Then there were the rest of us—the followers.

Or shall I say, Not leaders Yet.

But as the years passed, things started to change. I noticed most of us who were just followers in Professor Njoroge's class had finally evolved into leaders.

But how did it happen?

Maybe we were born leaders but had not yet (until then) used our leadership skills, or perhaps, as it turned out, we had been made leaders along the way?

After a decade of leading, I can confidently tell you this: *All leaders are made, and no leader is self-made.*

All leaders are made, and no leader is self-made.

Due to a series of happy accidents and hard work, I worked my way up into roles that entailed taking charge. There was no going back, and the only thing to do was to step up. I quickly learned that looks and labels are not the only things that make a leader.

It wasn't just about being in charge or having a loud voice. Instead, it was about having the right mindset and a set of skills and traits that anyone, regardless of age, gender, or size, could develop.

So, I began my quest for self-discovery and empowerment. Along the way, I encountered struggles and setbacks that put my leadership to the test. But, with each setback, I became more robust and determined to show that leadership had no limits.

All of us were born with the ability to nurture our leadership capacity through every single experience. These experiences can shape us to become leaders or followers at certain points in our life's journey.

In this book, I describe in detail the incredible experiences and life lessons that led to my transformation. I strip away the mask of strength and reveal the experiences that molded me into the leader I am today.

My goal in sharing my experience is to encourage and direct people from all walks of life to realize their full leadership potential.

Whether you are a young professional who wants to make a difference, a manager who wants to motivate your staff, or just a person looking for meaning and power in your life, then this book is for you. The concepts, tactics, and insights provided in these pages can help you become a leader at any level and discover that leadership is a force that can't be contained and that we hold the keys to it.

I cannot emphasize this enough: *The cost of being a great leader is self-leadership. It is the solitary factor that may catalyze your rise as a leader.*

In this life-altering adventure, I invite you to join me in questioning the status quo, ignoring the norms of society, and discovering your inner leader.

If you're ready to do so, let's get started.

*You are never too small to
make a difference.*

— Greta Thunberg

Part One:

Understanding the Leader's Mindset

=

"Mindset is what separates the best from the rest."

— Jo Owen

If there is one thing, I wish someone had told me earlier, it would be that if I had worked as diligently on my mindset as I did on the job, things would have changed for me more rapidly.

I wish someone had told me that if my actions reflected a leader's mindset, I would be more courageous and prepared to confront every aspect of the business game. And I wish I had known sooner that by training my brain to adopt a leader's mindset, I could direct the course of my career.

Think for a moment about the famous leaders you know, and you will realize that they may have varying personalities, leadership styles, and characters. Nonetheless, they all share a leadership mentality. It is what gives them authentic influence and authority.

They don't wait for circumstances to change for them to act; they act regardless.

They don't just act regardless; they inspire and empower others with their actions.

They don't just inspire others; they become role models.

They don't reach the top as easily as apple pie; they build a mindset stronger than their ego.

So, if the mindset begins the leadership journey, how can it be shaped, trained, and enhanced?

When I realized I needed to focus on my mindset, I devised this straightforward formula:

Identify the problem +
Find a solution +
Present alternatives =
A leader with a growth mindset

In the workplace and in life in general, problems are inevitable. Many people will complain about what is not functioning, but few will consider alternatives. Few individuals will inquire, "How can I contribute to finding a solution?"

When this occurs, the mindset of a leader kicks in, instructing your brain to become aware of the problem, consider what should be done, and act accordingly.

And when you discover a solution, you must also consider alternatives and train your mind[ii] to be receptive to the possibility that someone else may have a superior concept or improvement to yours.

People will be drawn to you because of your problem-solving abilities if you have this type of leadership mindset, whether you hold a leadership position or not.

My ascent to leadership status began with a mindset shift.

Leading is nothing short of being the person whose mind is in the right place with the right intentions.

When I realized the above, I concluded that, you must:

- Have that "I can, and I will" mindset.
- Start where you are.
- Rise in the face of difficulties.
- Believe there is a way out of any situation.

It doesn't matter how old you are or which position you hold as you read this; it's never too late to adopt the leader's mindset.

If you limit yourself, then you have no right to tell others that they can accomplish anything they set their minds to. Start with yourself if you wish to lead others. You lead yourself first; you change your mindset first; you become disciplined first; then, naturally, leading others comes to you easily.

You are always one step away from becoming a better leader. The question is, do you have the right mindset?

When you think you're beaten, you are.
When you think you dare not, you don't.
When you'd like to win, but think you can't
It is a sure thing that you won't.
When you think that you'll lose, you've lost;
For out in the world, you will find
Success begins with a man's will –
It's all in the state of mind.
When you think you're outclassed, you are.
You have got to think BIG to rise;
You have to FEEL sure of yourself
Before you can win a great prize.
Life's battle does not always go
To the stronger or faster man;
But sooner or later, the man who wins
Is the one who THINKS he can.[iii]

A poem by Walter D. Wintle

Chapter 1:
Be Faithful In Little Things

"Don't wait for big opportunities. You can create small but wonderful ones by starting with what you have."
— Israelmore Ayivor

Bujumbura, Burundi, December 2009.

When I entered the stately, old building of Telecel, a subsidiary of Telecel Global, I was a recent college graduate with no experience whatsoever. It was my first day as an intern in the Administration and Human Resources division.

I was thrilled and apprehensive about working in a department where I was the only "kid on the block". The remaining youthful employees were primarily employed in commercial departments, including call centers, customer service, marketing, and sales.

I've always known that I learn more from older people, so it was only a question of time before I felt at home.

I arrived promptly each morning, prepared to perform any assigned tasks. I was neither fussy nor difficult, nor did I have a negative attitude towards my internship. Since I was not receiving a monthly paycheck, I used the pocket money my parents gave me to pay for my transportation to work.

Joining the nation's second-largest private company felt like purchasing an economy ticket and being upgraded to business class. I understood it was a tremendous privilege that required me to elevate my mindset to greatness, a challenge for which I was prepared.

Three weeks after I joined, I had the opportunity to spend some one-on-one time with my department's head during a staff party.

It was the last week of December, and the company had organized, as it did every year, an end-of-the-year party where employees and their families shared lunch, danced, and mingled.

As a member of the Human Resources and Administration department, I was naturally involved in coordinating the event.

That day, my department's director, Aline, noticed me while I was frantically assisting everyone with last-minute tasks. I was hands-on and meticulous, and I took care of tasks that were not assigned to me.

The Monday following the celebration, she invited me to her office.

She sat in the far-left corner, where her desk occupied almost the entire space.

I entered and sat down, wondering why Aline had summoned me to her office.

She was such a natural beauty, a blend of sophistication and intelligence that set me at ease immediately. Instead of feeling intimidated, as one might when entering the office of a new supervisor, I couldn't stop staring at her.

Her natural charisma and the way she spoke with authority and courtesy made her the most popular leader in the company.

She began a conversation with me and asked for my assistance in obtaining some information from the department.

I told her, "Let me work on it, and I will get back to you as soon as possible."

I departed her office, set aside all other responsibilities, devoted my lunch hour to it, and reported back to her the same day.

"You see, this is exactly what I needed. Something fast and well done, thank you so much, Iris!" she exclaimed enthusiastically.

I believe that this is when she began to cultivate a level of trust in me.

I did not realize the significance of my report until the data was used to restructure the operational process of the department.

It did not matter to me whether the assignment was significant or insignificant. If assigned a task, I would complete it to the best of my ability.

My supervisors' confidence in me grew with each new assignment. Then, only three months after joining the company, she assigned me to replace a colleague on maternity leave. Consequently, I would be responsible for the entire recruitment department.

If I hadn't been dependable in my capacity as an intern, I would not have had the chance to lead in such a significant manner.

Leading starts with taking care of simple tasks with great care.

The most common lie most people tell themselves is that they will care for the major things if they ignore the minor ones.

You might be smart, skilled, and experienced. However, how you manage simple tasks reflects the opportunities that you attract. Most individuals lie to themselves by ignoring the minor tasks in favor of the larger ones. Eventually, the energy they put into small tasks turns into major ones.

Your attitude is more important than the magnitude of the task at hand. Your work ethic and philosophy are more important than your title or rank.

You can choose to be faithful in the little things by:

- Doing the right thing for your name's sake (your name is a brand), and doing it right, even when no one is watching. Don't settle for mediocrity because someone else will assess your work. Nobody wants to check for your avoidable mistakes.
- Ensuring that you've done your research. Keep in mind that structure, content, and delivery are equally important. It can set you up for significant work opportunities; especially if you work in a competitive environment.
- Becoming aware that your modest contribution is a part of a bigger picture. If you are tempted to neglect minor tasks because they are inconsequential, you may overlook the larger objective.

I love the story of the janitor who met with the late President John F. Kennedy while he was visiting the NASA space center in 1962.

When the President met the janitor and asked him what he was doing carrying a broom, the janitor replied: "Well, Mr. President, I'm helping put a man on the moon."

How wonderful is it to feel a part of something bigger even when your position may seem insignificant, and your contribution not that important?

This man understood the assignment; he surely did not consider his work more or less important than others. He aligned his contribution with the vision.

Your potential is not limited by where you are. When you realize that your title does not define your potential, you are confident in your role and eager to take on more challenging tasks.

It doesn't matter what title you hold or how much money you earn. If you are trustworthy in the little things, you will be trustworthy in the big things. And if you are untrustworthy in little things, so will you be when you are given bigger things to handle.

Reflection Questions

On being faithful in little things:

- Am I as trustworthy with small tasks as I am with big ones?
- If my line manager sent my work to management/client without reviewing it, would I be proud of my work?
- Do I believe that my role contributes to the bigger picture?
- Do I believe that I'm more than my job title?
- Do I put in the hard work when people see me and do little when no one is around?

Chapter 2:
Do Not Shrink

"You are built not to shrink down to less but to blossom into more." — Oprah Winfrey

I was born in Burundi, and as African daughters and sons, we were raised in a culture and society that taught us to shrink in front of hierarchy.

From generation to generation, it has been ingrained in us. Many African politicians, parents, and educators uphold this legacy of colonized African nations.

We are taught to respect our elders, even when that respect is undeserved.

It is the sad story of our inheritance.
We pay the price by living inauthentic lives. Our voices are diminished, our opinions and ideas are disregarded, and our self-assurance is shattered.

This shrinking syndrome isn't subjective to African society alone. Most underprivileged, discriminated against, or vulnerable groups experience it too. It might affect immigrants, racial and ethnic minorities, the disabled population, isolated children, and abused women or men.

Beyond the disadvantages imposed by society, shrinking is personal rather than collective. It's when a lack of self-consideration manifests externally.

Your journey to becoming a leader, regardless of your heritage, requires you to break the toxic cycle of shrinking and feeling small in the presence of any authority figure: leader, parent, teacher, elder sibling, uncle, aunt, etc.

Breaking this cycle requires diagnosing what I call the "shrinking symptoms," such as:

- Changing your tone of voice when speaking to a higher authority.
- Having the reflex of bowing down when a leader passes by you.
- Avoiding eye contact.
- Accepting unrealistic demands from an authority.
- Not asking questions to clarify instructions given by an authority.
- Saying yes to all requests.
- Putting someone on a pedestal and idolizing them to the point where you feel so small in their presence.
- Running away from authority or avoiding them for no reason.
- Taking the blame for something you did not do when questioned by the authority.
- Holding or hiding the truth to avoid hurting the authority's feelings.

Respect for one another is essential, but there is a significant difference between showing respect for those in positions of authority and seniority and retreating to the point where we are paralyzed, unable to feel secure in ourselves, and unable to progress in life.

To become a leader, you must exercise your power to be seen and consider others as equals, regardless of their titles, backgrounds, or social advantages or disadvantages.

Chapter 3:
No One Is Coming

"The price of greatness is responsibility."
— Winston Churchill

I had been employed for two years at Telecel when I received an important call.

It was a freezing day in Nairobi, Kenya. I had requested a work leave to attend the East African University Leaders Conference.

My supervisor, Aline, called me during a break and inquired, "Hello, Iris. I was wondering if you would be interested in a more challenging position within the department."

"Can I think about it and get back to you?"

"Sure, take your time. I want to know your answer before I publish it externally," she said.

I was eager to work in that position, but I gave her the impression that I needed time to consider it.

When I returned to the office, we briefly discussed the position and her expectations; I began my new position immediately.

During that period, the organization restructured all job classifications and compensation schemes.

A few weeks later, when I saw my new position on the grading sheet, I was dismayed that it ranked near the bottom of the job grading list.

How on earth was that even possible? I was unable to comprehend it. My peers in sales who were at the same level as me made three times my salary. I didn't know much about Human Resources then, but I was certain something was wrong.

I pondered, "Should I ask, or should I just let it go?" The conflict raged within my mind.

After struggling with my thoughts for a few days, I took a few deep breaths and entered the office of my colleague, who led the restructuring process.

It was mid-afternoon, and he had just returned from his lunch break. I knew that the moment was perfect for the discussion.

I began to inquire as to why my position was rated so low compared to its impact on the organization.

He attentively listened before stating, "Iris, you are right. Your role is vital; however, you don't bring in sales. That's why your paycheck is lower, even though you have the same qualifications as your coworkers."

The outcome of that conversation was not what I would have expected.

I was disheartened as I left the office. I attempted a variety of strategies, but they were futile. Office politics disadvantaged me. I lacked motivation for a full week, and I observed that no one was coming to rectify the situation.

I was disappointed not only by the injustice but also by the fact that I was cornered. I refused to give less of myself because of the system's failures. That would be a violation of my belief system.

Consequently, I let it go and learned a valuable lesson:

No one is coming to save you!

It's so easy to look at your circumstances and see nothing but unfairness. It doesn't take much effort to complain about something.

- The salary that doesn't match the value you bring to the organization.
- The manager who takes credit for your work.
- The colleague who always finds a way to transfer their workload to your desk.
- The acknowledgement you don't receive after a job well done.
- The late night and early morning efforts you put in that no one sees or values.
- The colleague who borrows money and doesn't return it on the due date or keeps pretending everything is alright and doesn't acknowledge the debt.
- The family members look at you for a handout, even before you receive your paycheck.

I could go on forever. One problem after another.

Guess who is coming to free you from your problems? Get you a promotion? Resolve your work-life balance issues?

No one.

You've got to save yourself.

Sometimes saving yourself means either keeping your mind from thinking dark days are ahead or refraining from acting in ways that don't align with who you truly are.

It means being brave enough to express yourself in ways you haven't explored before and daring to make decisions your future self will thank you for.

It also means believing in yourself and betting on yourself. Sometimes saving yourself is an act of faith.

Before you start wishing you had someone's life or didn't have to go through the circumstances you are going through, remember Jim Rohn's words:

"Don't wish it was easier, wish you were better,
Don't wish for less problems, wish for more skills,
Don't wish for less challenges, wish for more wisdom."

It is preferable to acknowledge that problems will always arise, regardless of how prepared or unprepared you are. Moreover, you must acknowledge that you are wholly accountable for the outcome of what comes next.

Be your own hero.

Chapter 4:
C Is for Conquer Yourself

"Bravery is listening even when you don't want to hear it." — Alaric Hutchinson

Growing up, my family and I lived in Kinanira, a small town in Bujumbura, Burundi. We resided in an old 1960s-era house built for Belgian colonial military officers.

The neighborhood was strictly designated for the families of high-ranking military officials in the national army. The house we lived in was so old that large fissures appeared in nearly every room, forcing the occupants to evacuate.

My father moved us in anyway.

He had joined the army as an officer after returning from his studies in Belgium. He struggled to find subsidized accommodations for his family, but a comrade told him about this house.

My father was not timid.

It did not matter to him that everyone else was afraid to move into this broken-down house. He started the formalities immediately to move us in and reassured my mother that he would find ways to fix some damages. His way of conquering his fears was to bring us all along into his optimistic world.

And just like that, we packed our lives, left the house my parents were renting in Kinindo, and settled into the old, cracking, but free house.

The land was nearly 1,500 square meters, of which the garden occupied two-thirds. The house occupied around 250 square meters. It had only three rooms: my parents' room, the children's room (which my brothers and I shared), and a junk room, or rather, dad's archive room turned into a storeroom by mom.

Mom thought dad's oldest documents and materials were nothing more than dust collectors and didn't serve any other important purpose apart from an emotional one.

There were two huge mango trees in the compound. One of them was the closest to our backyard. My brothers and I could see the mangoes blooming from our bedroom window.

When it was the right season to pick the mangoes, I could hear my brothers sneaking out of the bedroom during nap time to pick them from the tree.

When the mangoes were ripe, I could hear my siblings sneaking out of the bedroom during their naps to harvest them from the tree.

I remember watching my brother and his friend climb the tree and asking my older brother, "Ammiel, please throw me a mango; I can catch it from here!"

"Ok," he said.

He wasn't the kind of person who argued or talked a lot.

Five minutes later, I was still waiting impatiently for that mango. That's when I started hearing some teeth grinding and chewing.

"Guys, are you throwing me one?" I asked with desperation.

"I'm just tasting to see if these are good first," my brother replied, amused with himself.

I kept waiting.

Suddenly, I observed yellowish mango skin that had been chewed falling to the ground.

Then more, and more, and more.

I could see my brother and his friend sitting comfortably on that large tree branch, savoring the juicy mango, while I observed with anger and disappointment.

I was too afraid to climb the tree, afraid to insult him and lose everything, and I was enraged that I was a girl.

"If I were a boy, I would have been out there too," I thought.

I was thinking of the last threat to use against my brother, desperately brainstorming how to threaten or motivate him to share.

That's when I heard a small voice in my head whispering, "Why don't you climb out there yourself?"

I experienced an abrupt surge of courage that I hadn't felt in mere minutes. Without hesitation, I moved my feet towards the tree in preparation for a climb.

The initial attempt was unsuccessful, as was the second.

It was as slippery as an eel.

I kept sliding off the tree and could feel the tree trunk scratching my skin.

I was so determined not to be a spectator of my own fate that I kept wrapping my legs around branches, one branch at a time, until I was able to grab the last edible mango.

Every bite felt different: like I deserved it, like I was rediscovering the taste of it, like the wait was over, and I had attained my reward.

I savored that mango, and when I was done, I turned to my brother and his friend and said, "Thank you. Now this tree holds no more challenge for me."

That day, I overcame my own obstacles and changed my perspective from "I'm a girl" victimhood to a "I can do this" mindset. I was not only able to take pleasure in the fruits of my own labor, but the experience also changed me.

I do not know what is preventing you from pursuing your goals, but one thing is certain: you must first conquer yourself.

Do you want to conquer whatever is holding you back?

Here are the top five steps to overcoming your fears :

1. Do not blame anyone else.
2. Just do it scared.
3. Keep moving forward, especially when you start hearing negative voices telling you that you can't.

4. Welcome failures as part of your maturation process.

5. Keep your eyes on the prize and keep trying until you become a champion.

Many people today are stuck in low positions, living unfulfilled lives, hiding behind masks out of fear. Conquering yourself is possible. I realized it when I was a kid, and I still practice this today when I am in environments that require me to conquer myself, even as a leader.

The battles we fight are not always outside. Frequently, they reside within us.

Every time I take an opportunity to speak, even when I know I'm not the best speaker in the room, I conquer my fear of rejection.

Every time I have an uncomfortable conversation with a colleague, I conquer my fear of conflict.

Each time I take a chance on myself, I am conquering self-doubt and self-sabotage.

All of us have it within us. No one is above the other except the one who is not trying.

Make a promise to yourself: never fear to conquer, and never conquer out of fear.

Chapter 5:
Let Everyone Else Be Mediocre But Not You

"If you're always trying to be normal, you will never know how amazing you can be." — Maya Angelou

Starting my career in a highly competitive and demanding industry like telecommunication was a fire baptism. It was an introduction to workaholism - to working harder, not smarter.

Don't misunderstand me, both are important—hard work and smart work. You can't have one without the other. You must think hard before you can start thinking smart. And you must work hard first, before you can work smart.

Smart work is often the result of hard work.

I was fortunate enough to realize early on that there would be no smart work without hard work. Eventually, my own hard work led to smart work.

Hard work and smart work leave no room for mediocrity.

Mediocre refers to something of average quality, or something that is not very excellent.

In his book *'An Enemy Called Average'*[v] , John Mason defines mediocrity as follows: "Mediocrity is a region bounded to the north by compromise, to the south by indecision, to the east by past thinking, and to the west by a lack of vision."

From the moment I was appointed in my first role, I knew exactly how I wanted my work to be described: *anything but average.* I desired to be exceptional and outstanding, and there was a price to pay for that to happen. I had to put in hard work.

Some practical ways I developed a spirit of excellence were:

- Becoming detail-oriented: proofreading documents as if something were wrong.
- Offering solutions: helping colleagues meet their deadlines.

- Developing a self-taught mindset: teaching myself new things that could advance my work, doing online research.

These simple habits were sufficient to instill in me a non-mediocre character, which became my signature as I rose the career ladder.

Eventually, I attained a formal leadership position, a CEO position, and "Never be average" remained the foundation of my leadership rise.

Let everyone be mediocre, but not you.

This is the first piece of advice I gave my newly employed assistant after a minor incident made me realize that if I did not intervene, she could turn out to be average.

It was the middle of the week, and she had just joined the Human Resources firm I led in Kigali, Rwanda.

I was required to sign an essential letter at approximately 5:15 p.m., nearing closing time, when I did so. After I signed it, she gave it to a team member responsible for delivery.

When I contacted my assistant to confirm that the letter had been sent, she informed me that a colleague would deliver it the following day. The reason for this was that it was nearly time to return home.

I invited her into my office, closed the door, and then delivered my speech against mediocrity. *"Let everyone else be mediocre, but not you."*

I knew I didn't want her to be the type of person who settles for mediocrity, doesn't go the extra mile, or just does things by the book. My remarks were concise. I believe she noticed the disappointment on my face.

She left my office and delivered the letter that same evening. And from that day on, she has only strived for excellence in everything she does.

She understood that she could choose to step up if others were unwilling to do so. She realized that she could either offer an explanation or propose a solution.

A lackluster action does not make you or I mediocre; mediocrity as a system does. When you are mediocre, the repetition of average work becomes your way of life.

Being exceptional requires practice. It is a state of mind that requires you to do a little bit more than you intend to do daily.

Indecision and a lack of vision are the full package that leads to mediocrity.

Reflection Questions

On not accepting mediocrity :

- Do I often make excuses about the quality of my work?
- Do I give out my power by giving less than what I can offer?
- Do I nag a lot about what people are not doing when I could change something?
- Do I have a clear vision of where I want to be?
- Do I have the attitude it takes to get there?

Key Takeaways

Leading your way up requires a great deal of courage, bravery, and excellence, qualities we all have within ourselves. It's a mindset shift from "I'm small" to "I'm going to stand tall." From "I'm going to chicken out" to "I'm going to conquer myself and move forward with my fears."

Remember, all you need to do to lead your way up is to practice the five mindsets of leaders, intentionally.

1. Choose to **be faithful in small things**. Most people have a tendency to be serious about the bigger tasks and neglect the smaller ones. Choose to stay consistently great at your work, no matter the job title or responsibilities you have. Make it a lifestyle and see how many doors it will open for you. Think of being faithful in the little things as the key to unlocking big opportunities.

2. One thing I can assure you of is that even the most intimidating, powerful, rich, inspiring person you know has flaws. We're all humans, so **don't shrink** to anyone or feel small because we are all flawed. Belittling yourself is not being humble, and being humble is not about shrinking. Chanel that fear into the practice of what you'd say, how you'd stand, and how you'd measure up to that impressive person.

3. Identify what you need to do to start making things happen for yourself, because **no one is coming** to help you. As you

help yourself first, you will attract more opportunities, more growth, and more support.

4. Conquering yourself is more challenging than advising others to conquer their fears. Learning to **conquer yourself** will make you unstoppable and lead you to places you've never thought you'd be. It will uplift your mind and spirit and boost you into leading your way up.

5. Every time you are tempted to act in a mediocre or average way (remember, all leaders experience that too), speak out the choices in your mind and always choose the hard but rewarding way. Every choice counts, so make it count. **Let everyone else be mediocre, but not you.**

Now that we've covered the leader's mindsets, let's explore how self-leadership can make you an outstanding leader.

"The quality of your decisions determines the quality of your life."

— Tanya Taylor

Part Two:

The 7 Steps to Self-Leadership

"Mastering others is strength; mastering yourself is true power."

— Lao Tzu

Let me ask you a question: What's your power?

When you look at yourself in the mirror, do you see yourself as a leader?

You may think, "Iris, I see only one person in this mirror, with no one to lead." What are you referring to?"

You are correct. In this mirror, there is only one person visible. But can you see the multitude of individuals who reside within you?

We all have a committee in our heads that tells us what to do and what not to do, how and what to feel, which opportunities to pursue or abandon, and whether to act or stay still.

I want you to take charge of the mental leadership of the committee. The voices that put you down, that place more faith in others than in yourself, that prevent you from beginning because you are not prepared or because you lack funds, or support from your partner, family, coworker, etc.

Your biggest enemy in leading your way up is yourself. Your real power lies in mastering the committee in your head by:

- Increasing your self-awareness.
- Investing in developing your skills and competencies.
- Giving yourself the respect you want others to give you.
- Working on becoming more disciplined.

- Not waiting on others to give you more care than you give yourself.
- Regulating your emotions and affirming yourself in good and bad times.

Practicing all the above transforms how you relate to yourself and others and gives you the power to be a fulfilled version of yourself as a leader. The opposite is true as well.

Lack of self-mastery and self-leadership is the way to self-misery.

The day I realized this was the day my life turned around. I had already developed the five mindsets of a leader, but I still had little awareness of the impact self-leadership would have on me and the people I led.

I thought my power was in leading others, not necessarily leading myself. I believed so much in the servant leadership style that I had the wrong interpretation. I mastered the art of *leader-sheep*, not leadership.

I led a team of hundreds, and with my human resources background, my leadership style revolved around people. I naturally found my self-worth in helping and serving others.

But how could I possibly serve others if I didn't serve myself?

The answer was simple, but not straightforward. I used the servant leadership approach wrongly, and it hurt me, bringing frustration and disappointment, which caused me to feel exhausted and look at leadership roles only as a "hot seat."

I was appointed to lead a huge firm at a critical time, where I had to make crucial decisions to cut expenses, restructure, and motivate the team. I believed in transformation and wanted to change the less-performing team members, push them to become a better version of themselves, and help them unlock their potential.

I put aside the work I had to do on myself and invested more time and energy in wanting to lift and lead others. I helped some of my team members, and it was exciting to watch them unlock their potential as leaders.

Unfortunately, that small success delayed my realization that I was only responsible for changing and leading myself.

As leaders, our role is to be great masters of ourselves and to inspire others to be great masters of themselves too. Our role is NOT to lead others, but to lead ourselves so well that others feel empowered to lead themselves too.

That's how we make more leaders, not followers.

Everyone is their own leader first.

Everyone can improve their self-leadership. You can improve yours too.

Everyone is powerful. You are, too, because you are your own leader.

Everyone can lead their way up. You have what it takes inside.

All it takes is intentionality to develop the 7 Steps of Self-Leadership that I will share with you in the next few pages.

Chapter 6:
Self-Awareness

"To know yourself, you must sacrifice the illusion that you already do." — Vironika Tugaleva

It was a bright Monday morning, and my children were going to school. The sounds and voices of school preparations had been supplanted by silence. I felt compelled to use that time for introspection before diving into my new-week and new-goals mindset.

Typically, I record in my journal the things I'm thankful for and the areas where I want to improve. That day, I opened the Excel spreadsheet containing my strengths and areas for improvement so

I could identify a single area to focus on for the upcoming week. Then I had an "aha!" moment of realization.

What if self-awareness is more than knowing your strengths and weaknesses?

I have always known what I'm good at and what I'm bad at. In that way, I would have considered myself self-aware.

For example, one of my strengths is being a great networker. I genuinely enjoy meeting new people, interacting, and building connections. In the same area, one of my weaknesses is having a not-so-diplomatic face. I was raised not to give negative feedback verbally, and as a result, I unconsciously developed facial expressions that have betrayed me more than once.

If I disagree, you'll see it on my face; if I'm dissatisfied, you'll see it; and if I'm unimpressed, you'll see it on my face. It has not always served me well, particularly in leadership positions.

My creativity and ability to see the result or the broader picture are additional examples of one of my strengths. This has benefited me in numerous ways because I can articulate the vision and provide concise explanations.

However, my weakness is my inability to articulate the small steps that lead to the big picture or my lack of patience when someone explains an idea to me step-by-step, as I can easily grasp the big picture from the introduction.

Therefore, I tend to be impatient and encourage my team to get to the point, which makes me feel less like an empathic listener.

Most leadership books and conferences I've read or attended focus solely on strengths and weaknesses when discussing self-awareness and taught me to focus on the same. As I continued to examine my Excel spreadsheet, I reflected once more, *"There must be more to self-awareness than knowing one's strengths and weaknesses."*

- What if self-awareness means knowing which of our thoughts serve us and which do not?
- What if it's knowing how to use our time to our advantage?
- What if it's knowing which talent we have and using it to our advantage?
- What if our strengths and weaknesses are the result of the quality of our thoughts, and positive thoughts bring positive results?

Then I said to myself: "Iris, that's your answer."

That's how I developed the Three Ts of Self-Awareness:

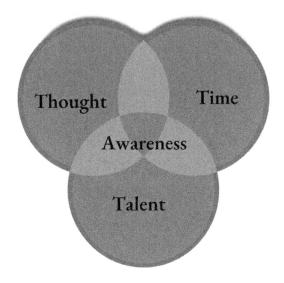

Self-awareness for a leader comes in these three areas, being aware of the quality of your thoughts, analyzing how you spend your time, and using your talent wisely. Let's break them down.

Thought Awareness

Something you'd never guess about me is that I am not optimistic—unless I force myself to be so. I often wonder how people like my father do it. How is every glass they see half full?

There are numerous reasons to think negatively. The mere act of turning on the television or scrolling through social media is sufficient to derail your day and thoughts. Wars, poverty, increased unemployment, crime, illness, and mortality are pervasive.

COVID-19 taking over the world and forcing us to remain at home and do everything remotely, it was easy to believe that life is unjust and not worth living.

I get it. I have those thoughts too—more than anyone in my own circle might imagine of me.

It is normal for us to experience melancholy moments characterized by intense negative emotions. It's how humans are hardwired. The positive and negative go hand in hand.

Being self-aware of the nature of your thoughts, or what your mind is engaged in, is a crucial aspect of self-leadership.

The ability to control one's thoughts and steer them in the direction of constructive actions or thoughts is what sets great leaders apart.

The day I discovered the American Reformed Theologian Karl Paul Reinhold Niebuhr's Serenity Prayer, I had an "aha" moment:

"God, grant me the serenity to accept the things I cannot change, the courage to change the things I can, and the wisdom to know the difference."

I realized, after meditating on the quality of my thoughts for some time, that I was constantly anxious about something negative occurring, whether at work or with my family.

Ordinary situations, such as boarding an airplane, attempting to close a business deal, or trusting a new or laid-back employee, prompted me to think, "What if something bad happens?"

I realized that these thoughts frequently caused me to be unconsciously worried and concerned about my life. My thoughts were focused on an unfavorable future, and this required modification.

I desired to have peaceful, courageous, and discerning thoughts. However, that was not my experience. Instead of tranquility, I was anxious and agitated from within. Instead of having confidence, I felt insecure. Instead of being genuine, I was powerful on the outside and broken on the inside.

The prayer for serenity altered the character of my thoughts, particularly at work. Every time I felt compelled to control a situation I had no control over, I recited the Serenity Prayer and soothed myself with two words: **Let go.**

Here are a few questions I started asking myself to be more self-aware and to elevate my thoughts using the serenity prayer:

On the serenity to accept the things I cannot change :

- Am I thinking about something I do or do not have control over?
- What are the facts I can't change at this moment?

- Am I in an acceptance or resistance frame of mind?
- Where should I redirect the thoughts of things I cannot control?
- How can I force myself to let go and let God?

On the courage to change the things I can :

- What am I capable of influencing? (*Example*: my thoughts, my frame of mind, my position, my foul language, and my fixation on things I cannot alter)
- What support do I need to navigate this challenging situation?
- Which people, places, or things should I reconnect with to uplift my spirit?
- Which action steps do I need to take to get myself unstuck?
- When was the last time I got myself out of a difficult situation? What was it like? How do I feel now that I'm reminded of that time?

On the wisdom to know the difference between what I can change and what I can't :

- Am I able to recognize that there is nothing I could have done to change this situation?
- How do I feel when I hang on to things I can't control?
- How do I feel when I focus on what I can control?

- What lessons am I learning from this difficult situation?
- What encouraging words would my best friend or trusted person share with me about this situation?

"All actions result from thoughts, so it's thoughts that matter."
– Sai Baba

Protecting your thoughts and being the guardian of your thoughts should be your priority. It is possible to increase the quality of your thoughts and elevate your life. You just need to chase away one negative thought at a time. Remember, what you think you become, what you feel you attract, what you imagine you create.

Be aware of what you think, feel, and imagine. The power is in your head.

Time Awareness

I was raised to believe that time is elastic. This was one of the most difficult things I needed to overcome as a leader.

African Time is, according to Wikipedia, the perceived cultural tendency in regions of Africa towards a more relaxed attitude towards time. This phrase is sometimes used in a derogatory manner to describe tardiness for appointments, meetings, or events.

I was raised in the culture of "African Time". Until I began working and realized the correlation between time and excellence, I didn't care much about time in everyday life. To avoid being typical, I learned to be time-conscious and to arrive early to make the most of each day.

My work was so demanding, I convinced myself that working on one thing at a time was not good time management. I got good at multitasking. Every time I had an idea or a task to do, I would open a new window on my computer.

Eventually, I had more windows open on my computer than I could possibly work on. It wasn't until recently that I became aware of how much stress all those open windows unknowingly created in my mind.

What I believed to be effective time management turned out to be ineffective. It had a negative impact on my time and productivity because I was constantly transitioning from one task to another without completing any of them.

I also discovered that I used it to prove to myself that I was too occupied for a social life or "me-time." I was unable to schedule leisure time or even a break because my computer and agenda indicated that I had too many unfinished duties. Each day, I closed some windows but opened others, and I rarely turned off my computer.

Becoming aware of how you spend your time can influence the habits you let in or let go of as you become a self-master.

Time is probably one of the most precious things we have. Sometimes we spend it wisely. Other times we waste it, lose track of it, or spend it on things that don't matter. We give it to others selflessly or guard it zealously.

No matter our habits, the clock ticks.

To be a good steward of your time, you must first recognize that it is a gift and a scarce resource. By doing so, you can organize your day in accordance with your life goals.

Questions to ask yourself to become more aware of your time :

- What habits do I have every morning?
- Who do I spend my time with?
- Which Apps do I spend more time on?
- Do I spend more time thinking or doing?
- Am I just busy or productive with my time?
- Do I schedule leisure, rest, and fun, or simply work?
- What time do I feel the most productive? Unproductive?
- How much time does it take me to unlearn a bad habit?
- How much time do I allocate in working on myself? My dream? My ambitions?
- Do I spend time multitasking as opposed to getting one thing done at a time?

People frequently ask me if I have 48 hours in a day because I accomplish so much despite having a demanding profession, being a present mother, partner and friend.

The truth is that I have less than 24 hours. I am probably *productive* for a total of six hours per day, spread out throughout the day. I experience emergencies, distractions, and interruptions just like everyone else. But when I realize, I'm veering off course, I typically count backwards from five to get back on course.

Jim Rohn beautifully advised: *"Don't spend major time on minor things."*

If you spend a significant amount of time on major things, like most leaders do, you will reap better fruits.

Don't forget that every dream you have deserves the best of your time.

Talent Awareness

Five to ten years ago, I never would have anticipated that I would possess the talents I have today.

Can you predict why?

I did not have adequate exposure to attainable talents. I sharpened my axe as I labored in various fields and sought new experiences.

Finding hidden talent is not always simple, but it is a game-changer. A discovery that sets you apart from the crowd is discovering a skill or trait unique to you.

It is simple to identify your innate skills. However, through practice and experimentation, many individuals uncover or develop latent abilities.

That's how I discovered mine.

I also know that sometimes it takes being told which talents are out there so you can identify one that sounds like you.

Here are some examples of leadership talents that can be used in the corporate world:

Talent list	Ways it manifests
Problem-Solving	Having the ability to be proactive and find win-win solutions.
Brainstorming	Thinking outside the box to expand thought and bring innovation.
Teaching	Being able to explain complex things in a simple way.
Researching	Collecting information through different channels to bring light or result in a particular topic.

Multilingualism	Being able to learn and speak new languages fast.
Public Speaking	Standing in front of crowds and being able to express yourself confidently.
Negotiating	Finding a way to move forward in tight situations and negotiate the best outcome.
Positivity	Being the source of comfort when things get tough.
Networking	Being able to captivate people's attention and forge valuable and enduring connections.
Active listening	Being able to care for people in a way that makes them feel heard and seen.
Agility	Being adaptable in different circumstances with different people.
Motivation	Boosting people's morale.
Add your talent here	*How does it manifest?*

These are but a few of the talents you might have now or might someday have.

The list is not exhaustive.

Here are a few questions to ask yourself to find out your talent:

- What are the things you would do free of charge?
- What activities make you lose track of time?
- What tasks do you naturally do without being asked?
- What are things people ask you to handle often?
- What do people usually thank you for?

Once you know what talent you have, put it to use because it's your unfair advantage.

Remember knowing and doing are two different things. Many people have talents they don't use, and that stops them from leading their way up.

If you want to use your talent, you will find a way.
If you don't, you will find an excuse.

Choose to use your talent to sharpen yourself and help others. An unused talent is as good as nothing. Self-awareness is the first step to becoming a great leader.

Take a minute and think about the great leaders you know.

- Do they master their thoughts?
- Are they mindful about how they spend their time?
- Do they use the talents they have?

If you answered yes to each of these, then you know they are using their self-awareness to their advantage. Do the same.

Applying the **Three T's** is a process and a crucial step in leading your way up.

Chapter 7:
Self-Development

"The swiftest way to triple your success is to double your investment in personal development."
— *Robin Sharma*

Every successful person you will encounter is engaged in some form of personal development. Regardless of how hectic their daily schedules are, they find time to engage in activities that contribute to their personal development.

There are three things I believe are directly tied to self-development.

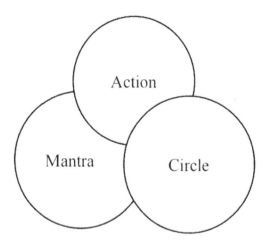

A learner's mantra, topped with action and the right circle of people, determines how successful they can be. These three concepts aren't shortcuts; rather, they're ongoing processes that yield lasting results for success. Self-development is an investment that shapes your future. It's the primary reason why it's important to commit to it in the present moment.

Shaping the mantra of a learner

When I was a teenager, I believed that obtaining a degree and graduating from university would be the conclusion of my educational journey. I yearned to complete secondary school, earn a bachelor's degree, then a master's degree, and be finished with my education.

When it was time for me to finish my A level, my father decided that at least one of his five children would study in an Anglophone system. His ambition was realized when he sent me to a Cambridge school in Uganda, as he cherished the English language.

Therefore, I began my A level studies in a foreign country while attempting to adapt to a new environment and channeling my inner strength to pursue my ambition of getting the best degree so I could be admitted to a medical university (a fact I had not yet disclosed to my parents).

It was a huge risk for me to pursue such an ambition, as failure would have meant taking out loans and incurring unnecessary debt. Even though it wasn't a calculated risk on my part, I chose to proceed.

I asked the principal to transfer me from literature classes to science classes, and he did so because I appeared to be a serious and disciplined student.

The first day of science class hit me like a punch in the face. It was physics, and I was eager to do something that demanded initiative. I had hoped to catch up swiftly, but what transpired was nothing like I had anticipated. I did not comprehend a single word of what was occurring. I am serious. When I surveyed my surroundings, I felt out of place. Every student was a nerd.

With fewer than ten students in the classroom, it was easier to spot the lost sheep.

Me.

I buried my head in my notebook and pretended to solve some math problems. I was writing a wish letter. It read: *"I hope I can find a student to be my tutor. Everything sounds Chinese. God send me a translator."*

I could converse well in English; that wasn't the problem. The problem was understanding scientific vocabulary and conventions. When it came to symbols, quantities, and units, I thought, *"There should be a dictionary just for naturally bad students like me."*

I didn't fully comprehend Newton's laws of motion or Hooke's law of elasticity, but I was determined to bluff my way to success. Eventually, the semester ended, and the results of my efforts were, well, not particularly impressive.

I did not receive a zero, but it was close. The fact that I got a 10% average in all of my science courses was a clear indication that I was about to give myself and my parents a heart attack.

I went back to the head teacher and requested a transfer back to literature classes. I was done playing with my education and understood that my job was to get better at what I was already naturally good at.

But something about me permanently changed. The more I studied and obtained a new degree, the more I realized how little I knew. My curiosity and desire for self-improvement increased with each degree I earned.

I ultimately obtained an MBA and realized there was little correlation between education and personal growth.

No matter how much we think we know, there is always something we don't know.

Education can sometimes shield us from self-development. It creates a finish line with a reward attached to it. That's why you will see leaders who don't want to improve, change, or learn from others, because they believe they have the highest level of qualification: diplomas and degrees.

In his book, Ego is the Enemy[vi], Ryan Holiday wrote, "The pretense of knowledge is our most dangerous vice because it prevents us from getting better."

Especially when it is nourished by education, familial status, position, background, etc., ego can impede personal development.

The first step to self-development is embracing the leader's mantra, acknowledging that you will never know it all.

This leads to openness, empathy, and an appetite to work on yourself, as opposed to finding explicit reasons to believe there is nothing to improve or work on yourself.

The second step to self-development is to understand the qualities you can and cannot get from education as you become a better version of yourself. Some things can only be learned in real time, in the real world.

The third step to self-development is identifying any areas in which you need to develop.

Here are some examples of self-development areas any leader should work on:

- Facing our fears: We can all develop the capacity to do things even when they scare us, because that is where growth happens.
- Mastering the art of conflict resolution: We can all practice rational conflict resolution. Problems are present everywhere—at work, school, and home—and they follow us everywhere. Most of us avoid conflicts instead of learning amicable ways to check our egos, face the challenge, agree to disagree, and move forward.
- Listening to feedback: It's not always easy to stay composed when getting feedback, but listening without interrupting or defending ourselves is something we should all practice more often.
- Staying calm under pressure: This is a whole level of emotional intelligence during a crisis that only a few leaders possess. It's natural to let your emotions come out, but when you can't control them, that is a sign of poor emotional intelligence.

- Developing communication skills: In a world that requires us to express ourselves more than ever, communication is no longer enough. You can work on and improve the art of persuasion.

Becoming action oriented

Have you ever had a great idea about a new skill you'd like to acquire or a new class you'd like to take, then watched the opportunity to learn it slowly fade away because you did not act on it when it was still hot in your mind?

Knowing you need to learn more, and acting on it are two different things.

In my experience in the HR department, I have truly seen that many people have the appetite to learn more but fail to act because they have excuses. One I've heard a lot is: "I don't have time for a new course, I'm busy with work."

Let's be practical and use these action steps to see how you can use five minutes to take action to develop yourself today:

Actions	Examples
Identify an area of personal development	Self-Confidence
Identify why this area is important to you	It will help me become a confident leader with better communication skills
Define the first action to be taken	Start a success journal in which I will write down all the big and small milestones I have each day
Determine which action should come next	Share with one person who looks up to me how I achieved this milestone. As I teach, I will learn more and practice self-confidence

Actions	Examples
Identify an area of personal development	Negotiation
Identify why this area is important to you	It will help me achieve my monthly sales target
Define the first action to be taken	Search for online certification
Determine which action should come next	Register and take the course. Ensure I find a mentor or class buddy with whom I can bounce ideas off

Act when the idea is still hot.

If you are thinking of one area where you need to develop yourself as you read or listen to this, pause for a minute, and move that idea from your head to a paper/phone so you can act later that same day (no later).

Action, fueled by the right mantra, breeds more results than thoughts. Act now, don't wait to be ready or to feel ready.

Building The Golden Circle

Leaders are humans. Like everyone else, they have a family, childhood friends, colleagues, acquaintances, and a small circle of trustees. This last group is what I call the golden circle.

You know it's a golden circle when the size goes low, and the value goes high.

The people in this golden circle have many characteristics in common:

- Transparency: These are people with whom you never feel the need to hide your truth. They encourage you not to feel ashamed to share.
- Honesty: They tell you the truth even if it hurts your feelings at that moment. They share unfiltered feedback with love and kindness.

- Trust: You have a space where vulnerability breeds understanding and empathy and where trust is mutual. You can seek their advice without fear of judgment because you trust them.
- Respect: You highly regard them because they've earned your respect through their actions, words, and lifestyles.
- Reliability: You know you can count on them to be there for you, not every time you need them, but every time it's important.
- Knowledgeable: You learn something new (small or big) every time you engage with them.
- Low maintenance: You don't have to talk to these people every day to feel connected to them, yet every time you converse, your relationship grows stronger.

In his book, *Think Like a Monk*[vii], Jay Shetty suggests, "For every negative person in your life, have three uplifting people." This is why it's so critical to select and delete from your golden circle anyone who doesn't better you. Keep them in your friend zone, not your golden circle.

Inside a Leader's Circle

Let's talk about a leader's circle at work. When I started my career, I noticed a couple of people at work who used to hang out a lot with my boss.

They always walked in her office with little or no access requirement; they spent evenings working on projects together, could talk on the phone for a long time, sometimes did sports activities together, etc. It only hit me when I became a formal leader and had my own circle that my former boss had always had one as well.

It was almost the same pattern, my golden circle were the people I trusted with work, spent much time with, and felt the most connected to.

One day, one of my closest colleagues genuinely asked me, "Don't you think your staff notices that you have preferred staff members?"

I paused and said, "True. I hope they notice and get the motivation to join the circle. It's not closed to them, but access is limited."

And this has always been my philosophy. Everyone on my team knows what it takes to join my "gladiator's team," my golden circle.

Let me share with you some criterias leaders look for in their staff before they make them a part of their golden circle:

- Able to anticipate problems/needs and take initiative
- Fast thinker and doer
- Selfless
- Can take and give feedback
- Bold

- Teachable
- Involved
- Passionate

Things leaders don't care about:

- That you don't have the qualifications to do it
- That you are new to the team or organization
- That you are still a junior
- That you look or sound different

These four things will not penalize you from getting into a true leader's circle. Just remember to get going, get good, and do not shrink.

Questions like the ones cited below can be excellent conversation starters when you are around a leader.

Don't shy away from asking these questions; save them, memorize them—whatever you must do to catch the attention of a leader, do that.

Conversation starter questions	Examples
To discover more about the leader	What was your first job? Which leader has impacted you the most, and why?

To discover more about their work	How did you find your passion?
	Do you have a morning or evening routine?
To discover more about their influence	Which leader has impacted you the most, and why?
	How do great ideas come to you?

If you know a bit about the leader, customize these questions and make them more personal.

Curiosity is a good virtue to have, especially when around great leaders. It is how we learn, develop, follow the footprints of inspiring people, and step into our destined great life. As a leader, it's an opportunity to feed people's curiosity with inspiration and share a bit about your Mantra, Action, and Circle.

Chapter 8:
Self-Discipline

"It was character that got us out of bed, commitment that moved us into action, and discipline that enabled us to follow through." — *Zig Ziglar*

The night before my parents sent me to boarding high school in Uganda, my mom called me from her favorite couch in the living room.

"Iris, I need to speak with you, come here."

"I'm almost done packing, Ma. I'm coming," I said, exhausted. I knew I was about to have one of those long conversations where she was going to give me all her motherly wisdom.

As I walked into the living room, she tapped the couch with her left hand and said, "Please have a seat here."

I was mentally preparing to accept everything she said, even if I disagreed, to shorten the conversation as much as possible. My only wish was to get to bed sooner rather than later, as my ride from Bujumbura to Kampala was scheduled for 6 a.m. the next morning.

It was around 10 p.m. when she started her Ted Talk, as I liked to call these sessions. I sat down and leaned my head toward her as if to say, "I'm all ears."

"My daughter, you are about to leave your parents' house to live in a foreign land with strangers. Your life is about to change. You will no longer be a little girl. I know you will do the best you can in school, as you have always done. But I want to share with you this advice that my father, your late grandfather, shared with me. "Nze numve mwananiwe namashure, sinze numve mwananiwe nindero."

Translated, this means, "I can tolerate hearing that you failed in school, but let me not hear that you've failed with discipline."

I nodded yes as she continued.

"Don't follow the crowds, don't let anyone influence you to adopt bad habits, don't be seduced by material things. You are special; act like it, and God will bless you. Let's pray."

She prayed for me longer than she had ever done so.

We hugged, exchanged smiles with watery eyes, and kissed goodnight.

When I left home that next morning, I couldn't stop meditating on her words.

My mom had never been one to care much about my grades. Discipline was the only thing she cared about, personal discipline, and I knew more than ever that my grandpa's legacy had lived with her. She was passing his wisdom on to me as I moved on to live a new life away from her sight and reach.

To my mother, discipline meant two things in particular: not being lazy and not living beyond your financial means. This made her a hard worker and a wise spender.

I started practicing self-discipline when I reached boarding school. I had 200 dollars of pocket money to manage for three months. That wasn't a lot compared to my classmates, who sometimes had thousands of dollars per term.

When their food budgets were replenished every month, I knew mine wouldn't be. I got into the habit of being content with what I had, never asking my parents to send me more so I could be like every other kid.

I remember one day one of my friends discovered I didn't have enough pocket money for the month and asked me, "Why are you pretending to have enough when you don't?"

I smiled and replied, "It's not the quantity that matters but the discipline to manage well, the little that I have."

I imagined my mom tapping me on my shoulder and saying: "I'm proud of you, ma fille."

Choosing the uncomfortable journey, whether in life or the workplace, is a key sign you are practicing self-discipline.

When it comes to self-discipline, you are your own enemy, and that's why you've got to make that extra effort to master yourself.

D is for Decision

One of the hardest things to do is decide to do the right thing for yourself. Making the decision to adopt a new habit or drop an old one, whether you like it or not, is discipline.

There is a difference between deciding (firm assurance that you are going to do something) and hoping to decide (which is wishful thinking).

Decisions are tough to make. That's why many people find themselves in unhealthy relationships, with jobs they don't enjoy, and with habits that don't serve them. It's easier to know what's not working for you than it is to take action to change it. This requires a higher level of discipline.

Becoming more disciplined is possible, but you've got to be hungry for more. There's got to be a price to pay and a reward to get. You've got to embrace the suffering that will help you reach your reward. It's simple, but hard to do.

To assess your level of self-discipline, you've got to analyze what you're disciplined at and what you aren't disciplined at, yet.

For example, I'm now disciplined about not mixing work/family time, which I worked towards. I leave work at nearly the same time every day and do not work on the weekends. I take that time to unplug from work and recharge to feel ready to tackle the week.

I'm trying to be in better physical shape since I tend to neglect my physical health in favor of my mental and spiritual well-being. I need to practice self-control by maintaining a regular schedule for going to bed, working out, and consuming water.

To achieve any new discipline, I realized it required breaking it into small steps:

1. Clarify the new habit you want to adopt. *Example:* Going to bed on time.
2. Determine the cost to pay—less social networking.

3. State a plan to overcome challenges. When you start thinking about the impossibility of the new discipline, plan to turn off your mind and shut yourself up. Just go and do it without thinking twice.

4. Identify the starting point. Set a clock reminder on your phone.

5. Track the progress. Day one, check the box.

6. Celebrate each win. Call/text a friend and brag about it.

7. Document the first 21 days. Keep a journal to track your wins.

8. Reward yourself. Order a small gift and get it delivered to your home/office.

9. Check in on the new habit. Mark the habit as adopted and add it to your discipline board.

10. Share the new habit. Teach someone else how to be self-disciplined. Be an accountability partner. The more you share, the better you become at that habit.

Jim Rohn, one of my all-time favorite authors, said, *"We must all suffer two things: the pain of discipline or the pain of regret or disappointment."* [iv]

I want you to think about it. What is it going to be for you? Which pain are you willing to embrace? What's holding you back? Meditate on it with a pen and paper.

Once you decide what you want to be disciplined at and start embracing the pain that comes with it, determine the reward you'll work toward, and see how much greater it is than the pain.

Chapter 9:
Self-Respect

"True leaders always practice the three R's: Respect for self, Respect for others, Responsibility for all their actions" — Anonymous

We live in a world where many people, especially leaders, want to be and feel respected. When they don't get their opinions validated, their decisions followed to the letter, or their requests acknowledged and treated with a sense of urgency, the skies fall.

We all either personally know or have seen that type of leader.

In Africa, our culture teaches us how to be "respectful" towards others before it teaches us what respect is and how to apply self-respect. This builds a society of egocentric communities that impose respect as they climb the leadership ladder.

What is respect, and how can we define self-respect?

Respect is a feeling of deep admiration for someone, or something elicited by their abilities, qualities, or achievements. An example of respect is actively listening to someone's thoughts because you admire them.

Self-respect is defined as holding yourself in high esteem and believing you are good and worthy of being treated well. An example of self-respect is when you know you deserve to be treated right and, as a result, you treat others the right way.

Self-respect got me where I am today. From when I was an intern with no income to when I was confirmed in mid-level to senior roles, I have always had self-respect. I still remember the faces of my colleagues when they learned an intern had hired them.

They remarked that nothing about me interviewing them clued them into the fact that I was just an intern. They said I portrayed authority and inspired respect. I wasn't faking it. I have always had high self-respect.

High Self-Respect

Here are five ways you can practice having high self-respect:

- Say "No" when you need to.
- Express your needs.
- Understand that you are equal with everyone else—not less, not more.
- Accept your weaknesses and strengths.
- Extend grace to yourself when you fail.

Low Self-Respect

Here are five signs of low self-respect you should avoid at all costs:

- Pretending to be someone you are not.
- Breaking your own boundaries.
- Letting others decide things for you.
- Compromising your beliefs to please others.
- Putting yourself down for your failure or other people's failure.

Boundaries are Self-Respect

When I hear statements like, "I don't work during certain hours" or "I won't allow this kind of behavior", I know that's a leader with clear boundaries, and it's attractive. Boundaries help us avoid unnecessary conflicts and tensions and reinforce our serenity as leaders.

To lead is to set boundaries. To set boundaries is to say "No". To say no is to mean it. To mean it is to live by your values. Your values are how you lead.

The journey to self-respect and setting boundaries will demand that you trust your own judgment, speak up fearlessly, and maintain and reinforce the boundaries if need be.

Examples of things to say to make your boundaries respected as a leader include:

- I'm sorry I can't help now; my cup is full. I'll get back to you as soon as I can.
- Can we discuss this at 2 p.m.? I would like to focus on some of the tasks at hand.
- I have a full schedule today; could you refer to xxxxxxx for feedback?

Examples of things to say to make your boundaries respected as leaders in the making (followers):

- I'd like to finish this task before starting this new assignment. Kindly bear with me.
- I have a few other priorities now; should I reprioritize these other tasks?
- I've committed to finalizing this before jumping on another task; can you help me do that?
- This question is personal; can I respectfully pass?

Ownership is Self-Respect

Leaders make mistakes. Not just once, but many times. To lead is to fail at something, but knowing your failure doesn't determine who you are as a leader.

It's acknowledging and owning your mistake without feeling like a fraud or failure and extending the same kindness to yourself that you express to others who fail. It's being unapologetically gentle with yourself.

Most people can't openly acknowledge their mistakes because their self-respect is attached to their success. When you make mistakes and make amends, you inspire others to do so and create a space where mistakes are not taboo.

In my organization, "Lead Access", my colleagues and I encourage each other to fail fast and own it with these three mantras that are related to ownership/self-respect:

- In this office, we make mistakes and make amends.
- We learn from each other's mistakes.
- We win or learn together.

Wouldn't it be great to fully celebrate our personalities as we embrace leading ourselves and others?

Building self-confidence is ineffective without building self-respect.

Chapter 10:
Self-Regulation

"Live life as though nobody is watching; express yourself as though everyone is listening."
— Nelson Mandela

Every day can't be a great day. The more I became a seasoned leader, the less good days I had in a row.

Challenges and situations that require self-regulation surface more frequently than situations that don't. I often found myself on an emotional roller coaster, having to take a step back to self-regulate before my anger got the best of the situation.

And to be honest, some situations that made me angry shouldn't still be happening in the 21st century.

Leading has a cost; be humble and control yourself.

I once went to a particularly popular bank to add my signature as the official company representative. I was excited because I had been appointed as the Managing Director of one the leading HR firms in Rwanda.

I was beginning to implement numerous new changes, and I could sense the team's enthusiasm growing. It was difficult but promising.

That Thursday morning, I informed a former coworker and one of the bank's administrators that I would be passing by the headquarters to complete the documentation.

She informed me that the Branch Manager had been notified, and it wouldn't be long.

When I arrived, the receptionist asked me to wait in the lobby and informed the Branch Manager that I had arrived. The Branch Manager was on the phone but could see me through his office glass window.

Every time I have an appointment, I always carry a book with me just in case the person doesn't show up on time. It helps me regulate my impatience while doing something I enjoy and can learn from.

I had just picked up my book from my rose gold bag when I saw the Branch Manager put down his black office phone and walk towards me.

We introduced ourselves.

"Hi, my name is Iris, and I'm the Managing Director of ITM Africa," I said, shaking his hand.

"You are the MD?" he asked with a surprised and incredulous tone. "But you are very young," he continued.

"Oh, really? How old do you think I am? Quick hint: I am a mother of two kids," I added, trying to downplay the moment.

"No way. When did you have them? Where did they come from?" he asked, shamelessly referencing the shape of my body without thinking his questions were off-limits.

"Well..."

I paused for a second trying to decide if I was going to start a gender discussion with him, or if it was a waste of time and energy.

"I think we are all grown-ups and know the answer to that. There are always surprises when we judge the book by its cover. Back to business, can I sign the documents so I may run along for my next meeting?" I asked, all business.

"I still can't believe you are the MD and have two kids," he insisted while handing over the documents.

"Again??? You are not going to let this go, are you?" I questioned him in my head.

I smiled and then replied, "Many can't believe it, but there is a French saying that goes, *"Aux âmes bien nées, la valeur n'attend point le nombre des années"* which translates to *"To the well-born, value does not wait for the number of years."*

I looked straight into his eyes as I handed over the signed copy.

This is an answer I usually give whenever the patriarchs question my value based on my gender or age.

As I walked out of his office, the overthinker in me, fueled by anger, kicked in.

I was angry that it was the second time in the day that a man who didn't know me had the audacity to engage in an unprofessional discussion about my physical looks. It had happened a bit earlier in the day as well, during a meeting with board members of a client.

After I introduced myself and the team, one of the board members confidently and loudly stated, "Oh, you are the MD? I thought you were a model when you walked in."

Everyone laughed. Some found it funny; others found it unprofessional.

I felt embarrassed for him, but the evil voice in my head said, *Clap back.*

The angelic voice in my head was convincing me not to take offense and not to let my ego take over. If I responded in anger, all my preparation and the team's work would be for nothing.

I made the choice not to care and laughed along. And just like that, we were back to business as if nothing had happened.

Mastering Emotions

Self-regulation diminishes the ego, whereas self-deregulation applauds it. Leading is a humbling experience for the egos of leaders with high self-regulation. It is a skill of highly emotionally intelligent leaders.

When you intentionally nurture the art of keeping it cool when you feel attacked, or disappointed by someone's opinion of you, the power comes back to you.

Here is the formula I use when managing my emotions:

Pause + Reflect + Respond = Self-Regulation

There are many ways to practice self-regulation:

- You can remind yourself that you have options to choose from: Attack, Avoid or Affirm yourself. When faced with a tense circumstance, we frequently believe that our only option is to attack, but this is not the case. We can also evade the conversation or remark by disregarding or avoiding it. And we can affirm ourselves by permitting our internal monologue to remind us of our worth. Repeating these three A's can help you select an action that is consistent with your fundamental values.

- You can choose to take time before you act, speak, or engage. For example, you can use the balcony tactic for anger management (adopting a detached state of mind, allowing you to see the scene from a bird's-eye view). You can drink something to help you take a small break, use the bathroom, etc.

- You may also pay attention to the signals your body language sends you. For example, if you begin sweating, have shaky arms/legs, change your speech tone, or feel your pulse rate accelerate, these are all symptoms that you are entering a rage state.

There are three questions I often ask myself when I need to regulate my anger:

1. Will this matter in five years? Most certainly not.
2. Is this coming from a place of insecurity or hurt? When I identify what's what, I practice empathy.
3. Should I be the bigger person here? This reminds me of my values and encourages me not to react to people's darkness.

Leaders with high self-regulation can reap the fruits of this valuable human quality. Here is how they respond when a triggering situation occurs.

- They calm themselves when experiencing anger.
- They internally have positive self-talk.
- They do not avoid hard conversations.
- They keep an open mindset/growth mindset. They don't think they are the only ones who are right and everyone else is wrong.
- They know a bad situation doesn't make a bad person.
- They move on and don't hang on to anger.
- They don't gossip about it to attract hatred of the person, company, or situation.
- They bounce back and don't let the situation affect their mood.
- They practice self-compassion when they feel down.

Pay attention to how you solve problems. Do you do so in your head, do you break them down on paper, or do you share them with a trusted person?

I must confess. Self-regulation is a natural talent for me for a simple reason. I hate being the source of hurt for people. In my early days as a leader, especially in my junior and mid-level roles, I avoided conflict under the guise of self-regulation. You must not confuse self-regulation with avoidance, like I did. It leaves scars and robs you of the opportunity to be the master of your story.

Luckily, leadership roles exposed me to conflicts, and I still remember my heart beating fast every time I had to find a solution to arising conflicts with teams, partners, or clients.

Learning to fight well is a leadership quality. But picking your battles is another important quality to have as well.

How well you regulate yourself amid chaos speaks a lot about your leadership maturity.

Chapter 11: Self-Care

"How can we embrace rest and play if we've tied our self-worth to what we produce?" — Brené Brown

In many cultures, rest is not something that's celebrated.

Growing up, my mother used to tell me and my siblings that school holidays were not meant for sleep and laziness but for a change of activity. We knew we couldn't just sit around and do nothing, especially if she was around. We were privileged to have house-helps, so we didn't understand why mom would not let us just chill.

I remember walking towards my mom one morning while she was getting ready to go to work and asking her, "Ma, I suffered this term with unending homework, walking from home to school and back, helping my little brother with his homework when I was done with mine. Don't you think I deserve to just rest this holiday?"

"Did you not sleep last night?" she replied.

"Yes, Ma, I did."

"So, what are you talking about? That was resting. Now go and help Justine (our house- help); she could use an extra pair of hands."

I knew it was hopeless before I even spoke to her, but I figured, why not give it a try?

As a result, I learned to be "busy" every time my mother came back from work. In fact, my siblings and I pretended to be busy whenever we heard our parents' car approaching the house. From one kilometer away, we could tell by the noise of their respective car's engines, which parent was arriving home.

Because we were raised in a household (and a society) where we constantly had to prove that we were busy doing something, we now unconsciously criticize or shame ourselves for not being active. We convince ourselves to engage physically or mentally to feel a sense of accomplishment.

We don't necessarily differentiate being busy from being productive, but instead normalize getting active to prove our worth to ourselves and the world around us.

And we do not normalize taking a break or resting.

This impacts how we handle ourselves in the workplace, as well as how we judge ourselves and others.

When I first got into the corporate world, I noticed similar signs. When the managers came, everyone suddenly seemed to be so busy. When the boss was around, I almost never saw a coworker sip coffee and take a short break during the day.

A coworker pouring himself a cup of coffee and returning to his desk to drink it while they worked didn't seem strange. And it was very disrespectful to see a group of coworkers hanging out in the coffee area, drinking coffee, and talking about things that had nothing to do with work.

The pretending was so effective that colleagues would alter a non-work-related conversation to a work-related one and raise their voices to demonstrate to a supervisor strolling by that they were not simply taking a break but rather engaged in a working conversation over coffee.

Sound familiar?

In fact, the only colleagues who seemed to have earned a small break were:

1. The top performers, the stars in the office, confident in their value and what they brought to the table.
2. The non-conformers, employees who had mastered the art of not giving a ******, who feared no man, not even God.
3. The bosses, the men and women in charge who no longer had to prove themselves to anyone.

These three categories of people may understand their self-worth, but in fact, they exemplify self-esteem, self-acceptance, and self-assurance, not self-worth.

Let me explain.

- Top performers usually have high self-esteem, which is their overall opinion of themselves— how they feel about their abilities and limitations.
- Non-conformers have self-acceptance. True self-acceptance is embracing who you are without any qualifications, conditions, or exceptions.[viii]
- Bosses have self-assurance because of their titles.

Self-worth is a feeling of confidence that you are a good and useful person. It's that simple, although most of us have been brought up to think otherwise.

We must reprogram our brains and detach our self-worth from what we produce, which is incredibly difficult for most of us. We must consider our worth not for what we've achieved but simply for who we are—good people.

Top performers don't believe they have value simply because they are good and useful people. Their self-worth is rooted in their abilities (and limitations).

Non-conformers don't care if they are good or not. They are who they are. Take them or leave them. They simply do not care.

And bosses do not necessarily believe in their inherent value; they base their value on the rank and title they have achieved.

To practice good self-care, we must begin by believing in our self-worth.

Here are a few affirmations that can help increase our self-worth, especially in the corporate world:

- I'm a good person, and I'm deserving of all good things.
- I value my identity and past experiences but do not let them affect my self-worth.
- Working hard is not what makes me more worthy in my own eyes or in the eyes of the world around me.
- I'm confident that I'm a good person.
- I'm not worthless when I choose rest over work.

Perhaps you are wondering why I titled this part— "self-care"— when all I have talked about up to this point is self-worth? The answer is simple. Our ability to care for ourselves is deeply rooted in our self-worth.

If we are always trying to prove our worth by showing how busy we are, we will never feel worthy enough to rest. And rest is the foundation for good self-care.

Normalize Lazy Moments

The best leaders rest and normalize their "lazy" moments.

All leaders who truly understand the weight of their responsibilities know how important it is to invest as much in rest time as they do in work time.

There are only two categories of leaders: the exhausted leader and the rested leader.

The exhausted leader rarely delegates, and if they do, they are very hands-on and involved in the whole project, micromanaging the work and the employees until everyone else is exhausted as well. This leader never takes a break, never takes a day off, never takes a holiday, and has the same expectations of everyone on their team.

The rested leader trusts their team and therefore takes breaks, doesn't often work over the weekend, and goes on holidays (sometimes more than their team). They are innovators because their mind is rested enough to be innovative.

Exhausted leaders should never be applauded; rested leaders should be because they can think more clearly and are kinder.

Which leader are you?

Waiting to rest until there are no more problems to solve is like waiting for snow in the summer time.

Problems Will Still Arise

Problems will always be there; that's a fact.

As a leader, your priority is to know when to act and when to rest and let others take over. That can be the most difficult aspect of being a leader—not acting.

It feels like you are not caring enough, but the process of learning to back away and rest, even when problems continue to arise, is peace mastery.

When I was in mid-level positions, I believed I was a traitor for not canceling my time off when a crisis developed. My employer frequently told me, "No one is irreplaceable," which I knew was true to some extent. But I was also aware that when I outsourced significant duties, I frequently had to repeat them since my working standards were not always the same as those of my coworkers.

In those days, it wasn't easy to take my leave. I had to learn to be the type of leader who understood that rest was an important part of leadership.

The first thing I had to let go of was the idea that I was irreplaceable. Most people do believe themselves to be irreplaceable, whether consciously or unconsciously.

It can manifest in different ways:

- Delays in requesting leave days
- Canceling your leave for reasonable or unreasonable work emergencies
- Failure to delegate tasks efficiently
- Regular follow up on emails and work-related activities while on leave

Whether the reason for this thinking is professional conscience or the need to impress your employer, what typically lurks behind this behavior is the assumption that we are irreplaceable. I had to relearn how to properly enjoy my vacation by convincing myself that life continues, and business goes on, even without me.

The second thing I had to let go of was the idea that delegation was bad. I had this belief based on my reality. I have never delegated tasks before my vacation and found things done the way I would have done them, simply because no one is me.

No one will think the way you do, negotiate things like you, or make the same decision as you. It's unrealistic to think of delegation that way. You delegate tasks, not your thoughts, your workstyle, or your personality.

You must allow everyone to be who they are in the process, clearly explain what the end result of the task should be, and allow people to use their style, even if you may not fully align with it.

When I started viewing delegation as empowerment, it opened my eyes to the possibility that rest was still an option, even during crisis moments.

Having the ability to enjoy life, rest, laugh, and travel knowing your team will solve problems to the best of their ability (even if it's not the same way you would solve the problem) is what every leader should aim to embrace.

It's easy to think that you shouldn't rest because the world would stop without you, but think about this quote from Russell Baker: *"A solved problem creates two new problems, and the best prescription for happy living is not to solve any more problems than you have to."*

Problems will always exist. Choose which problems you will address yourself and which you will delegate to others. And take care of yourself since your worries will not go away.

Scheduling Rest is Scheduling Joy

According to the Bible, after six days of creation, God chose to rest on the seventh day. (Gen.2:2-3)

God must have known we weren't machines, that we would need to rest too. Most organizations offer some form of a weekend as a day off. But instead of becoming a rest day, the weekend is often filled with activity. Most corporate people, including myself, have weekly shopping to do, social responsibilities like birthdays or weddings to attend, sport activities in groups, side hustles, etc.

Although my weekend is not a typical workday, it often leaves me exhausted (as I imagine it does for you as well).

It wasn't until a year ago that I scheduled my rest day. Thursday is my day to rest like a goddess. I don't plan meetings on that day, and I don't engage in anything that requires physical or mental effort. I call it the joy day. It's the day where I intentionally take care of myself, buy myself flowers, rest, and do things at my own pace.

I like saying to my friends that on Thursday, the day doesn't run me; I run the day, unlike every other day of the week where I wake up with things to tick off my agenda.

I know it is a brilliant idea because every time I share this day with fellow leaders, their eyes shine with desire to implement it.

You may be asking if I took a day off on Thursday but still made my team work. The answer is no. Everyone on my team has a right to my "Joyous Thursday" now that I call the shots. On Fridays, we get together, eager to finish the week strong.

If your workplace is not flexible, you can still schedule rest and joy on your calendar. Do what you've got to do; I don't know what works in your life, so be creative, but find your day inside the weekdays. If you really can't find a day within the week, be intentional about how you spend the weekend.

Be unapologetic about your rest time. Schedule joy.

Chapter 12:
Self-Affirmation

―――

"You cannot control the behavior of others, but you can always choose how you respond to it."
— Roy T. Bennett

Don't expect people to affirm you.

In today's era, we expect others to affirm us, acknowledge our work, and lift us when we feel down. We seek to be heard, seen, and validated.

We get annoyed when we give way to the next driver who doesn't thank us for doing so, we feel disappointed when our bosses don't notice the small/big efforts we are making to push forward the work, we feel bad when our significant others don't notice the hairstyle change, new outfit, new scent, etc.

We are wired emotionally to care about what others think of us and ultimately crave affirmation, especially from those around us on a day-to-day basis. All that makes us the emotional humans that we are.

What's sad, however, is that no one teaches us to affirm ourselves. No one teaches us to praise ourselves so that we might not crave external praise.

Encountering Self-Affirmation

One cold Sunday morning, my Sunday school teacher began to tell us about God's love and asked us to repeat after her, *"I'm loved, I'm a child of God, I am wise, and I have a great future ahead."*

That was the first time I encountered self-affirmation.

The more I repeated it, the more I believed it. It was awkward to affirm myself. At first, it felt like I was bragging, then like I was a fraud. My late grandmother used to say that saying kind things about oneself (self-affirmation) builds the ego, but now I realize it's quite the opposite. It's other people's affirmations that often build our egos.

Affirming yourself is a soothing act, and declaring big things in your life when times are tough is an act of self-compassion.

Self-affirmation is important for leaders. It pushes away defeat, depression, pain, and suffering. It's the total opposite of self-sabotage, self-doubt, or self-destruction. It's self-construction. It's looking at the brighter side and projecting yourself there.

I love self-affirmation because it makes us see and feel what's possible. It's faith. It's not wishful thinking. It's a powerful declaration. You don't have to feel it to declare it, you just must put it into the universe.

It's important as a leader to source your strength within you so you can fill your cup and affirm others too. You can't give what you don't have. You can't affirm others if you can't extend that same attention to yourself. Even if you tried, it would be less fulfilling than knowing you are extending the same grace to others that you extend to yourself. Trust me, I was there.

There are many ways you can affirm yourself.

Some words you can use to affirm yourself for the good days at work are :

- I'm exactly where I'm supposed to be, and I'm grateful for it.
- I'm a badass human who shows up for myself and others.

- The effort and hard work are paying off. I'm proud of the leader I'm becoming. I'm part of something bigger than me. I'm walking gracefully in my life's purpose.
- My mental, physical, and spiritual needs are met. I'm special and deserving of all things beautiful.

Some words you can use to affirm yourself on bad days :

- No one is dying today, that's what matters.
- I'm prepared for the bad days. Nothing can take away my calmness.
- I'm not my situation, or challenges. I'm a problem solver.
- This situation, too, shall pass. My breakthrough is coming.

Some critical points to reflect on:

- What makes it difficult for you to self-affirm?
- When do you need self-affirmation the most?
- How can you develop this habit?

Key Takeaways

The 7 Steps of Self-Leadership can take your places, not just in your career, but in every aspect of your life, including relationships, if you commit to applying at least one of the seven steps to start with.

1. Use the Three Ts of self-awareness to get good then great at your craft.
2. Apply the M.A.C. (Mantra, Action, Circle) of self-development to expand your mind.
3. Decide how and what you need to take action with self-discipline.
4. Hold yourself in high regard to increase your self-respect.
5. Don't confuse self-regulation and avoidance; learn to pick your battles wisely.
6. Rest is your ultimate self-care practice.
7. Self-affirm and remind yourself how awesome you are.

"The most important thing is to try and inspire people so that they can be great at whatever they want to do."

— Kobe Bryant

Part Three:

Leadership is Not a Title or Rank

―――

If your actions create a legacy that inspires others to dream more, learn more, do more, and become more, then you are an excellent leader.

— Dolly Parton

In the year 2000, just when most of us were expecting the end of the world, my dad put on his beige army ceremonial uniform and peaked cap with a flag pin. Then he joined his promotion for the official decoration for a higher rank and title in the national army. It was such a proud day for him and us, his family, as we followed the ceremonies on TV news. It wasn't just a ceremony. It was a symbol of authority and signaled he was due the respect of soldiers in lower ranks, who were obliged to stop and salute him when he'd pass by them.

In the army, leadership was packaged with rank.

But, if there is one thing that I'm sure of today, it's that in the corporate world, leadership cannot be packaged in a job title. You can't command blind obedience to your team like in the army, it doesn't work like that.

The more you climb the career ladder, the more you realize that a leadership role is not a destination. There are two possible situations; move up as you intentionally invest in your growth, or freeze, thereby becoming stagnant as a leader.

Many leaders today are too concerned with titles or too busy with organizational quotas to be concerned about assessing their leadership growth or stagnancy.

One thing I can assure you, leaders who invest in themselves keep rising, and those who don't, feel miserable and depressed with the weight of daily leadership.

Leading your way up and staying at the top of the game requires thorough personal evaluation, including sitting with yourself and rating your skills and competencies in all aspects of your leadership life.

Self-leadership is the path to great leadership.

The Leader in Your Mirror

Remember when I shared with you about the leader in your mirror? What if we did a few exercises to uncover how they are doing?

If you are keen to discover the type of leader you are, let's get practical.

I have put together these thirty-five statements to help you find out which of the seven self-leadership steps you need to keep working on to become a better leader.

Use a pencil to circle the number that best describes your feelings in relation to any of these self-leadership statements. Be as honest as you can be.

Strongly agree = 5
Neutral = 3
Strongly disagree = 1

Self-Awareness	Agree 5 4 3 2 1 Disagree
I don't spend major time on minor things.	
I can name three things I'm talented at.	
I regularly get unfiltered feedback from others.	
I know what motivates me to get things done.	
When negative thoughts arise, I don't entertain them for more than five minutes, and then focus on positive thoughts.	

Self-Development	Agree 5 4 3 2 1 Disagree
I ask others for help as part of my self-development plan.	
I can name my top three areas of growth.	
The five people I spend the most time with help me develop the skills aligned with where I want to be.	
I don't enjoy staying in my comfort zone.	
I can spot and take on opportunities when they arise, even if I am not fully ready.	

Self-Discipline	Agree 5 4 3 2 1 Disagree
I usually meet my own deadlines.	
I have role models in terms of self-discipline.	
I can name the top three ways I waste my time.	
I can name three things I am disciplined at.	
When I make decisions, I change my mind just because it's difficult to get it done.	

Self-Respect	Agree 5 4 3 2 1 Disagree
I believe I am good enough.	
I have the power to stop myself being aggressive physically or verbally.	
I have the courage to speak up or leave any situation that disrespects and diminishes me.	
I am treated with respect and understanding by others.	
If I were to make a list of three people I respect the most, I would be one of them.	

Self-Regulation	Agree 5 4 3 2 1 Disagree
I can bring my attention to my breath when in a conflict situation.	
I am aware of what my negative triggers are.	
I validate the emotions I feel when triggered, I don't avoid them.	
I know how to take time to regulate and refresh my mind and body when I deem it necessary.	
I voice my concerns in a calm manner, even when I am upset.	

Self-Care	Agree 5 4 3 2 1 Disagree
I have a daily practice of doing something good for myself.	
I take regular breaks to clear my head whenever it's necessary.	
I can name three people, activities, places that bring me joy and refill my energy.	
I communicate my self-care needs to my entourage and enforce boundaries around my me-time.	
I don't neglect my health. I listen to my body and get check-ups with a doctor regularly.	

Self-Affirmation	Agree 5 4 3 2 1 Disagree
I practice positive self-talk.	
When I fail, I affirm myself the same way I would affirm a friend in need.	
Every time I see myself in the mirror, I'm proud of myself.	
I don't feel like I am a burden to my colleagues, friends, or family.	
I am able to accept myself just the way I am.	

Now that you have circled your score, get the sum of your score for each one of the seven self-leadership steps. The lowest score you can get for each section is 5, the highest you can get is 25.

Self-leadership area	Overall Score per section
1. Self-Awareness	
2. Self-Development	
3. Self-Discipline	
4. Self-Respect	
5. Self-Regulation	
6. Self-Care	
7. Self-Affirmation	
	(Insert Total Score /35)

Use your result to identify the area of self-leadership that you need to invest in. Embrace the M.A.C. (Mantra, Action, Circle) to make it happen, and always remember that growth comes in more shapes than we think.

Use different resources available to you to increase any of your lowest self-leadership behaviors.

Refining your leadership competency is part of the growth process. Don't fall for the analysis paralysis; just write down one thing you are willing to do while reading this book, and then act on it.

Ask any person in your circle to rate you on the above. Compare your score to see what others think of you. It could be an eye-opener and conversation starter when it comes to collecting feedback.

Don't wait to be empowered; rather, empower yourself.

As a leader, keep in mind that there is always someone doing something better than you. Learn from them. And there is always someone looking up to you. Teach them.

Know when to look back to find motivation and when to look forward for inspiration.

The 14 Habits You Need To Stop Now If You Want To Lead Your Way Up

1. Do not let anyone use/manipulate you, regardless of your position vs. their position.
2. Do not expect others to believe in you more than you believe in yourself.
3. Do not hang out with people who don't bring any added value to you. It doesn't matter if they are family, childhood friends, or church buddies; know when it's time to get on the next bus and move on. Your destination is not everyone's.
4. Do not trust people's words; rather, trust their actions. It's their commitment to you.
5. Do not depend on anyone entirely; stay alert. Teach yourself things and be the driver of your projects.

6. Do not wait for support to come to you through divine intervention. Know when you need support and ask for it. Know when you just need to get your mind right.

7. Do not assume you know it all. Be brave enough to acknowledge that you don't know everything and remain teachable. Do this even when you get a seat at the table.

8. Do not resent people for their bad behaviors or attitudes. It's a waste of time and energy. We are all flawed; all of us fall short. Learn to let go, to smell the roses, and to blow out candles (such a good breathing technique). Never hate anyone, even for stealing your project, taking away your promotion, badmouthing you, not sponsoring you, etc. Do not give away your power. Let it go. It's not worth it. Five years down the road, when you ask yourself if it still matters, it won't, I promise.

9. Do not lead to please others. Not even yourself. Lead to do what is just, to improve systems, and to leave people better than you found them. Sometimes it will look ugly, and you will suffer, but you know when just is just. Stick to that mantra.

10. Do not let your ego get in the way of the bigger picture.

11. Do not give up when things get tough, because trust me, they will. Ramble, curse, play your favorite music, drink your favorite drink, call someone—do what you must do to regroup and get back in the game. Leading your way up will put your physical, mental, and spiritual muscles to work. Get in the habit of selecting your battles and fighting the right ones with grace.

12. Do not turn a blind eye because it's not your department, task, or job to do. If you see it, fix it; don't just talk about it. Act.

13. Do not major in small talks, tasks, or things. Look outside the box, look at the challenges, the "not so easy work" and then choose that path.

14. Don't tell yourself "No". Let others do it. Often, we refuse ourselves opportunities because that little voice in our heads says, "No one will accept your project. Don't ask that question; it's too basic or dumb. Don't ask for that promotion, as there is no open position. Don't negotiate for a higher salary; they know you are jobless, new to the job, etc." Often, when we tell ourselves "No", we rob ourselves of a "yes" opportunity. Practice telling yourself, "I can take a "no" from others, but from me, it's a yes!"

Practice these new habits and unlearn the old ones. Continue to learn and unlearn even when you get a seat at the table.

Lead Your Way Up Alphabet

Do you have the characteristics of a leader on the rise? Place a checkmark next to the letters that represent you the most or circle the letter you want to work on.

A - Ambitious

B - Bold

C - Curious

D - Determined

E - Effort

F - Focused

G - Grateful

H - Honest

I - Informed

J - Joyful

K - Kindhearted

L - Loyal

M - Motivated

N - Noticeable (not average)

O - Objective

P- Patient

Q - Qualitative

R - Reputable

S - Selfless

T - Teachable

U - Understanding

V - Vulnerable

W - Wholesome

X - (eXcellence-oriented)

Y - Youthful

Z - Zealous

Leading Is Giving

The final goal of leadership is not self-interest. It should start with yourself and always end with others. When you become so good at mastering your craft, you become a catalyst for change and inspiration in people's lives. Giving becomes your currency as a leader. You are called to empower, serve, and be a giver of the resources that you are filled with. The question is, "What are you filled with?"

When your cup is empty as a leader, the outcome can be lost and frustrated followers. It can lead to personal breakdown, misalignment, and failure to make projects successful as a leader.

On the contrary, when your cup is full, the outcome is trusting and reassuring followers. It can lead to personal upliftment, alignment, and motivation to make projects successful. It is all connected. How well or poorly you lead others is connected to your capacity to lead yourself, fill your cup, and influence others by giving.

"Perhaps your quest to be part of building something great will not fall into your business life. But find it somewhere. If not in corporate life, then perhaps in making your church great. If not there, then perhaps a non-profit, a community organization, or a class you teach. Get involved in something that you care so much about that you want to make it the greatest it can possibly be, not because of what you will get, but just because it can be done." - Jim Collins[ix]

When all is said and done, people will remember what you poured into their cup and what your leadership style inspired them to be, feel, or do.

Will you lead your way up to share and care? I hope your answer is YES.

A Letter from Iris

Dear Reader,

As you come to the end of this book, I hope you've picked up something from the sum of my leadership doubts, wins, and lessons. I want you to know that, just like you, I'm still in the quest of defining and refining the leader I am because leadership is a long-life journey. It is a journey that does not end when you assume leadership. It persists even if you become the most powerful person in the room.

If I were to sum up my leadership experience, it would be the practice of leading yourself when no one else is following. That is what will inspire others to follow you, even if you are not a formal leader.

Leading your way up is a mentality that is not based on your past experiences, fears, or deficits. It is based on the future opportunities you are willing to grasp unapologetically or create for yourself.

What matters is not where you are coming from, but where you are headed. What matters is not the talent you have, but the talent you are sharpening.

What matters is not how many opportunities you've missed, but how many you are ready to catch from now on.

Your leadership style can get better if you get better.

So, dismantle your limiting beliefs, find a coach, a mentor, an accountability partner, and work harder on leading yourself than you do the people around you.

Remember, two, five, or ten years from now, you will land somewhere, and the question is, where is it going to be?

Will you be proud of your journey, or will you wish you had acted differently?

The truth is, whether you believe you can lead your way up or not, you are always right.

Bet on yourself and live in the power of self-leadership so that more people can be encouraged to lead their way up. Never fear to lead, and never lead out of fear.

As you start embracing your full potential, there will be times when you may doubt yourself, your vision, your ambition, or the sound of that unique voice you bring to this world. You might even doubt who would listen to your story or who would want to follow you.

The truth is, there is always someone learning from you, someone slightly behind you, someone lighting their candle from your light. That person needs you. Remember them when you think you are inadequate and turn your "mess into a message."

I want to share with you a passage that transformed the outlook I have on my life, a passage I've memorized for days when I have doubts:

Our deepest fear is not that we are inadequate.
Our deepest fear is that we are powerful beyond measure.
It is our light, not our darkness that most frightens us.
We ask ourselves, 'Who am I to be brilliant, gorgeous, talented, fabulous?' Actually, who are you not to be? You are a child of God.
You playing small does not serve the world. There is nothing enlightened about shrinking so that other people won't feel insecure around you. We are all meant to shine, as children do.
We were born to make manifest the glory of God that is within us.

It's not just in some of us; it's in everyone. And as we let our own light shine, we unconsciously give other people permission to do the same.
As we are liberated from our own fear, our presence automatically liberates others.

The words of Marianne Williamson are a reminder that there is room for all of us to be great leaders and shine our lights on the world.

So, quit playing small and shrinking, let your light illuminate, and give yourself a chance to lead your way up.

Within, you have all it takes to be a leader, but you will never have it all to lead. Embrace that truth and chase your goals with conviction that you will get further than your mind can grasp. And when you are reminded of what you lack to make it happen, know that the power to defeat your weaknesses is in your thoughts and your actions.

Keep Going, Keep Growing.

You got this.
With love,
Iris

Acknowledgements

No leader is self-made. I'm surely not self-made, and that's why I'm going to take this acknowledgment seriously.

To my sons, Nolan, and Eden, it's my prayer that you grow to lead yourself and take chances on yourself in every circumstance. I will keep building a safe and challenging space for you to learn, grow, and evolve.

To my resilient and wise mother, Jeanne. You've always been a self-leader, a quiet force, and a self-starter. I learned from you the best lessons on integrity, dignity, sacrifice, and survival. Thank you for loving me with my imperfections and allowing me to use my voice to share my thoughts from a young age.

To my charismatic and loving dad, my Bishop and General Onesimus. Thank you for being a role model and life teacher.

To my brothers, Ammiel and Eben, without you I wouldn't be the resilient Iris I am today. Thank you for challenging me and creating space for me to level up and think tactically.

To my sisters, Sarah and Michelle, you are the reason I wore the hat of the role model without necessarily asking for it or being ready for it. Being your big sister and little mama did not come naturally to me, but I want you to know that if I were given a chance to choose my sisters, I would still choose you.

To my personal cheerleaders, Aniella Beaulier, Aline Mutambuka, Erica Mbanda, Dorcas Rutunda, Gaelle Nsengimana, Faith Keza, Allegra Nduwimana, Rama Keto, Jatinerida Evora, thank you for being the wind beneath my wings. Your unwavering love, encouragement, and loyalty has carried me through triumphs and tribulations and I'm forever grateful to each one of you.

I want to thank my accountability partners in this project: my dearest Habibah Waziri, from leading together, being challenged together, traveling for work together and later for fun, you've been a truly amazing friend with purposeful conversation with the perfect dose of humor and fun. And thank you for gifting me books that inspired me on my own journey as a writer and for always allowing me to borrow a book from your shelf.

To Anemone Basabakwinshi, partner in growth for her time, precious and personified advice and words of wisdom that always left me stunned. Thank you for your intentional friendship, mentorship, and guidance, and finally, Louise Umutoni Bower, for the push to get finished when I felt stuck. Thank you for encouraging me to not settle for anything other than the dreams I have. I'm thankful for the tribe the three of you became on this journey.

A special thanks to my editors, Carol Jones, for believing in this book from the first call, and Ivan Nyagatare and his team for bringing my vision of the book to reality.

And most importantly, I want to thank you for picking up this book and spending your precious time journeying with me in these few chapters. I imagined each one of you when writing this, and honestly nothing brings me joy more than sharing my experience with you.

It's my hope that you find a portion of the answers you need to start or continue your journey to self-leadership. I promise you I will be here to cheer you on, motivate you, and reaffirm you when you need a friendly ear.

About the Author

Iris Irumva is a seasoned business leader, entrepreneur, executive advisor, speaker, and author with a proven track record of success in the corporate world. With a wealth of experience managing teams of over 1,000 people in East Africa, she has established herself as an authority in the fields of Human Resources, Leadership, and Career development.

Born and raised in the beautiful country of Burundi, Iris did not consider herself a natural-born leader, so she focused on being the best follower. However, her journey took a transformative turn when she was presented with opportunities to lead and excel.

Through sheer determination and unwavering commitment, Iris rose through the ranks, ultimately earning prestigious positions in renowned organizations such as Telecel Globe, the International

Organization for Migration (UN) and ITM Africa, showcasing her ability to adapt and thrive in diverse environments.

She is currently the Founder and CEO of Lead Access Ltd, a consulting firm with a mission to empower leaders at all levels through coaching and mentoring. With an MBA from Oklahoma Christian University in the United States, Iris combines her academic knowledge with real-world experience to offer practical and effective solutions as an ICF-certified Coach.

Her focus on fostering positive work environments, developing leaders, and driving organizational growth has made her a trusted and respected figure in the industry.

Her unique techniques have made her a sought-after speaker at various workshops, conferences, and events, inspiring others to embrace their leadership journey, challenge societal norms, and advocate for gender equality in leadership roles.

Beyond her professional accomplishments, Iris is also a dedicated mother of two, striking a harmonious balance between her career and family life.

Website: irisirumva.com
LinkedIn: Iris Irumva
Twitter: Iris Irumva
Instagram: IrisIrumva

Sources

i   Kari Keating et al. Developmental Readiness for Leadership: The Differential Effects of Leadership Courses on Creating "Ready, Willing, and Able" Leaders. Journal of Leadership Education, October 2014.

ii   "To Be a Great Leader, You Need the Right Mindset." Harvard Business Review, September 13, 2021. https://hbr.org/2020/01/to-be-a-great-leader-you-need-the-right-mindset.

iii   Winkle, Walter D. (1905) Thinking. Unity Tract Society, Unity School of Christianity.

iv   Rohn, J. (2017, December 26). "Jim Rohn Quotes Don't Wish it Were Easier, Wish You Were Better." YouTube. Retrieved July 6, 2022, from https://www.youtube.com/watch?v=8yG7N9NrQ8c.

v   Mason, J. (2013). An Enemy Called Average. Insight International.

vi   Holiday, R. (2016). Ego Is the Enemy. Profile Books.

vii Shetty, J. (2020). Think Like a Monk: Train Your Mind for Peace and Purpose Every Day. Simon & Schuster.

viii Sussex Publishers. (2008, September 10). "The Path to Unconditional Self-Acceptance." Psychology Today. Retrieved July 30, 2022, from https://www.psychologytoday.com/us/blog/evolution-the-self/200809/the-path-unconditional-self-acceptance.

ix   Collins J, (2001), Good to Great, Why Some Companies Make the Leap and Others Don't. Harper Collins Publisher.

Printed in Great Britain
by Amazon

42057433R00086